CONTENTS

ABOLISH CHILD SUPPORT

Written by J.E. Warner

CHAPTER 1: OVERVIEW OF THE CHILD SUPPORT ENFORCEMENT AGENCY

Overview of the Child Support Enforcement Agency

In 1975 Gerald R. Ford signed into law a section of the Social Security Act that established a national child support collection system. Ford's own father was assigned child support and did not pay, Ford expressed his "concern" with the federal goverment intervening in domestic relationships, but signed the bill anyway.

On September 7, 2024 the house approved 405-18, legislation (H.R. 4678) designed to streamline the child support collection system. The women's congressional policy institute played a crucial role in passing this legislation. (There is no men's congressional policy institue, if you were wondering.)

Under the bill, states would be allowed to review and update child support orders when custodial parents leave the welfare rolls, and at least every three years moving forward. States would be encouraged to increase their use of information in the federal New Hires database for locating noncustodial parents who have not complied with child support orders.

The measure would expand a program that allows the denial of passports to noncustodial parents who owe child support. Currently, passports can be denied for those with $5,000 in outstanding arrearages; that threshold would be dropped to $2,500 under H.R. 4678. Similarly, the bill would allow the denial of visas and residency status for those owing $2,500 in child support.

The Child Support Enforcement Agency (CSEA) was established with the intention of helping custodial parents secure financial support from non-custodial parents. Designed to alleviate poverty, reduce reliance on public assistance, and ensure a stable environment for children, CSEA's mission is noble in theory. However, many argue that its practices and impacts have deviated significantly from its initial goals.

The Origins and Evolution of CSEA

The roots of the CSEA go back to federal mandates aimed at reducing welfare dependency by ensuring that non-custodial parents contributed financially to their children's upbringing. Originally, the system was structured to pursue parents who could afford to pay but chose not to. Over time, however, the agency's focus shifted toward aggressive enforcement policies that, in some cases, have led to more harm than good for families involved.

Establishment of Federal Support: Federal support for child support enforcement began in earnest with the Social Security Act amendments in the 1970s. These changes required each state to create an enforcement system to establish and collect support payments.

Shift in Focus: While initially focused on securing payments from parents who were intentionally avoiding their responsibilities, CSEA gradually broadened its scope to include automated collections, wage garnishments, and even punitive measures for non-payment.

The Agency's Modern-Day Practices
Today, CSEA uses a variety of measures to enforce child support payments. These range from income withholding and interception of tax refunds to more severe actions such as driver's license suspension and incarceration. Critics argue that these practices can undermine the financial stability of non-custodial parents and create a cycle of debt and punishment that harms families rather than helps them.

Financial Injustice: Critics argue that CSEA's one-size-fits-all approach does not account for the unique financial situations of non-custodial parents. Impact on Mental Health and Family Dynamics: Constant enforcement pressure, wage garnishments, and the threat of punitive measures often strain family relationships. Lower-income non-custodial parents are disproportionately affected by strict enforcement measures. While criticisms are mounting, some advocate for a more balanced, supportive approach that still ensures child support without punishing the non-custodial parent harshly.

CHAPTER 2: THE EVOLUTION OF CHILD SUPPORT LAWS IN THE U.S.

The Origins of Child Support Legislation: A System Meant for Different Times

Child support legislation in the United States emerged in the early 20th century as an effort to ensure that children received adequate financial support, particularly when parents separated or divorced. However, the social and economic realities of that era were vastly different from those of today. Initially, child support laws were created with good intentions, targeting non-custodial fathers who neglected to provide for their children's well-being. But as societal structures evolved, so did the reach of these laws—transforming them into something that many now see as outdated, unjust, and fundamentally harmful.

A Tool for Reducing Welfare Dependence: In the 1970s, as part of the welfare reform movement, child support enforcement became a federal priority. The government believed that by enforcing child support payments from non-custodial parents, they could reduce the financial burden on welfare programs. Child support was no longer just a family obligation but was politicized as a way to address poverty on a national scale.

Shift from Assistance to Enforcement: What began as a tool to alleviate poverty morphed into a punitive mechanism. States were incentivized to collect child support, even in cases where the non-custodial parent faced financial hardships, leading to aggressive enforcement actions that often disregarded individual circumstances.

Enforcement Policies: Criminalizing Poverty and Hardship
The primary issue with the evolution of child support laws is that they do not account for the economic disparities and changing realities of non-custodial parents. The one-size-fits-all approach treats poverty as though it were a crime. By using stringent enforcement policies, the system is essentially punishing parents for being poor or financially unstable—often trapping them in cycles of debt and even incarceration.

Driver's License Suspensions and Employment Barriers: The irony of child support enforcement measures is that they often prevent individuals from earning income altogether. Suspending driver's licenses for non-payment is a common practice, but it does nothing to improve the financial stability of the non-custodial parent. Instead, it creates further barriers to employment, making it nearly impossible for them to fulfill their obligations.

Incarceration for Non-Payment:
 Perhaps the most controversial enforcement tactic is jailing parents who cannot pay. This does nothing to help children or custodial parents and instead costs taxpayers, while further destabilizing families. The practice criminalizes poverty, disregarding the fact that most individuals in arrears are genuinely unable to meet the high demands imposed on them by the system.

The Role of States in Intensifying Enforcement
Since the 1980s, states have received federal funds based on the amount of child support they collect, creating a system that incentivizes aggressive enforcement regardless of actual ability to pay. Rather than tailoring enforcement to individual cases, states often pursue all non-custodial parents with equal vigor, whether they are "deadbeat" parents or financially struggling individuals who need assistance rather than punishment.

Quota-Based Enforcement:
 State agencies are often under pressure to meet certain collection quotas to secure federal funding. As a result, the system prioritizes revenue generation over the well-being of children and families. In some cases, even minimal amounts of child support debt can trigger extreme enforcement actions, as the goal becomes simply to extract money rather than address the underlying needs of families.
Impact on Low-Income Communities:
 These aggressive policies disproportionately impact low-income communities, exacerbating financial instability and perpetuating cycles of poverty. The threat of enforcement can force parents into under-the-table jobs or discourage them from working altogether, out of fear that every dollar earned will be siphoned by the state.

The Reality of Child Support Debt: A Never-Ending Burden
One of the most severe consequences of current child support laws is the accumulation of arrears—unpaid child support debt that grows over time due to interest and penalties. For many parents, this debt becomes insurmountable, and even after the child becomes an adult, the state can continue to enforce collection. This creates a lifetime of debt for some non-custodial parents, with no realistic pathway to freedom from financial hardship.

Interest and Penalties: Child support debt often accrues interest, sometimes at rates as high as 10% or more. This means that even if a non-custodial parent is making consistent payments, their debt can continue to grow, creating a permanent state of financial stress and insecurity.
Inescapable Debt: Unlike most debts, child support obligations cannot be discharged through bankruptcy. This policy traps parents in financial hardship with few avenues for relief, regardless of changes in their personal circumstances or ability to pay.

The Broken Logic of Child Support Laws: Why Reform Isn't Enough
The underlying logic of current child support laws is based on the assumption that non-custodial parents are financially capable but unwilling to support their children. In reality, many non-custodial parents are simply unable to pay due to their economic circumstances. By ignoring this fact, child support enforcement laws create more harm than good, placing children at the center of a punitive financial system that burdens both parents.

Flawed Assumptions: The enforcement system operates under the assumption that all parents can afford the set child support amount. This assumption fails to consider fluctuating income, job instability, and other financial hardships that are especially common in today's gig economy.

Erosion of Family Ties: By turning child support into a government-enforced debt, the system often creates resentment, division, and long-term harm to family relationships. Non-custodial parents who are pursued relentlessly by enforcement agencies may become estranged from their children, undermining the very purpose of child support.

A Call for Abolition: Beyond Reform
It is increasingly clear that reform alone cannot address the fundamental issues within the child support enforcement system. Advocates for abolition argue that it is time to dismantle the current model and explore new approaches that genuinely prioritize the welfare of children without criminalizing parents who are struggling financially. Ideas for a more equitable system include community-based support programs, direct assistance for custodial parents, and income-sensitive policies that take a holistic view of family needs.

Alternative Support Programs: Community support initiatives could provide assistance to custodial parents without the need to pursue non-custodial parents through punitive measures. These programs could include employment services, housing assistance, and educational grants to empower parents directly.

Direct Financial Assistance for Families: Providing financial support directly to families, rather than relying on non-custodial parents to make payments, could help address the needs of children more effectively while reducing conflict between parents.

CHAPTER 3: UNINTENDED CONSEQUENCES OF ENFORCEMENT

Introduction: The Collateral Damage of Aggressive Child Support Policies

Child support enforcement is ostensibly meant to ensure that children receive financial support from both parents. However, the unintended consequences of the system reveal a much darker reality. As enforcement agencies focus increasingly on punitive measures, they often create more problems than they solve. In many cases, these enforcement actions disrupt the lives of parents, foster resentment, and, ironically, can even reduce the financial security of children. This chapter examines how the unintended fallout from child support enforcement policies undermines families, damages relationships, and perpetuates cycles of poverty.

◆ ◆ ◆

1. Financial Insecurity for Non-Custodial Parents
One of the most common unintended consequences of child support enforcement is the financial devastation experienced by non-custodial parents. Far from encouraging compliance, aggressive enforcement can plunge non-custodial parents into poverty, making it even harder for them to contribute meaningfully to their children's lives.

Wage Garnishment and Asset Seizures: Child support agencies often rely on wage garnishment and asset seizures to collect payments. This tactic may secure some funds in the short term, but it can create severe financial hardship for non-custodial parents, especially those already on a tight budget.
Cycle of Debt: Once enforcement starts, it's difficult for many non-custodial parents to escape the debt cycle. If they miss a single payment due to unexpected expenses or a temporary job loss, interest and penalties compound quickly, leading to a debt load that grows faster than they can pay.
Reduced Employment Opportunities: Aggressive enforcement measures can lead non-custodial parents to avoid formal employment altogether, especially if wage garnishments make it difficult for them to survive on what's left. This creates a vicious cycle where non-custodial parents may turn to under-the-table jobs, diminishing their financial stability and career growth.

◆ ◆ ◆

2. Psychological Stress and Mental Health Consequences

The stress of dealing with child support debt and constant enforcement can have significant mental health consequences. Non-custodial parents report high levels of anxiety, depression, and even suicidal thoughts as they face an overwhelming system that feels impossible to escape. The stigma and shame associated with enforcement can lead to social isolation, further worsening mental health outcomes.

Shame and Social Stigma: Non-custodial parents subjected to enforcement measures often feel like societal outcasts. The stigma of being labeled a "deadbeat" parent can isolate them from their communities and even their families, creating psychological harm and eroding their sense of self-worth.

Chronic Anxiety and Depression: The relentless pressure to meet financial obligations under threat of punishment can cause chronic mental health issues. For some, the weight of this burden is so intense that it affects their ability to work, parent, or engage in daily life, further harming the family unit.

◆ ◆ ◆

3. Damaged Parent-Child Relationships

One of the most tragic consequences of the child support enforcement system is the way it damages relationships between non-custodial parents and their children. Children often become collateral in the battle over payments, leading to strained or even estranged family relationships.

Resentment and Alienation: When non-custodial parents are forced to comply with aggressive enforcement measures, they may come to resent the custodial parent or, unfortunately, the child who is "causing" their financial hardship. This resentment can translate into distance, anger, or withdrawal from the child's life.

Reduced Contact with Children: The stress and financial burden associated with enforcement can make it difficult for non-custodial parents to spend time with their children. Travel expenses, legal fees, and reduced income from garnishments all limit a parent's capacity to maintain a close relationship, creating a barrier between parent and child that grows wider over time.

4. Impact on Custodial Parents and Children's Financial Stability
While custodial parents are often assumed to benefit from enforcement, this is not always the case. Enforcement actions can backfire, making non-custodial parents less able or willing to contribute financially, thus reducing the intended support for children. The high cost of enforcement actions often redirects resources away from the families who are supposed to benefit from these payments.

Administrative Costs Eat Into Support: State agencies collect billions of dollars annually through enforcement actions, but a significant portion is diverted to cover administrative expenses. This means that families often see only a fraction of the funds collected on their behalf.

Negative Impact on Children's Financial Support: When non-custodial parents face financial penalties or job loss, the total amount of support available to children decreases. Instead of creating financial security, enforcement policies can lead to fewer resources for children.

5. Racial and Socioeconomic Disparities in Enforcement

The child support enforcement system disproportionately impacts low-income and minority families, creating a cycle of disadvantage that reinforces systemic inequality. Enforcement measures are often harsher on parents from marginalized communities, leading to a disproportionate number of penalties, incarcerations, and wage garnishments among low-income individuals and people of color.

Targeting of Low-Income Non-Custodial Parents: The enforcement system is particularly harsh on low-income parents, who are often the least able to meet high child support demands. By focusing on punitive measures instead of support, the system perpetuates poverty in already vulnerable communities.
Racial Inequities: Studies show that minority non-custodial parents are more likely to face punitive measures, which exacerbates existing economic and social disparities. For Black and Latino communities, this means higher rates of incarceration and job loss due to unpaid child support, further entrenching systemic inequality.

6. Incarceration: A Counterproductive Solution

Jailing parents for non-payment of child support is a controversial practice that does little to actually secure financial support for children. Instead, it creates a series of cascading problems that harm families and communities.

No Benefits for the Child: Incarceration removes any possibility of financial support since incarcerated parents are unable to earn income or make payments. This outcome does nothing to help the child and often leaves custodial parents in worse financial situations than before.

Taxpayer Burden: Imprisoning parents for unpaid child support costs taxpayers millions of dollars every year. These funds could be redirected toward more constructive programs that actually help families, instead of perpetuating cycles of punishment and debt.

Conclusion: Unintended Consequences as Justification for Abolition

The damaging consequences of child support enforcement policies provide a compelling argument for abolishing the current system. Instead of protecting children, these policies create barriers, foster resentment, and fail to provide meaningful support for families in need. An overhaul of child support policies —moving away from enforcement and toward community-based solutions—offers a far more effective and humane approach to supporting families.

By focusing on reducing poverty, providing job support, and ensuring financial security without punitive enforcement, society can foster a healthier environment for children and parents alike. The time has come to acknowledge that child support enforcement, as it stands, causes more harm than good, and a different approach is desperately needed.

CHAPTER 4: IMPACT ON NON-CUSTODIAL PARENTS

Introduction: The Unseen Burden on Non-Custodial Parents
Non-custodial parents are often portrayed as negligent or irresponsible, a narrative that fuels the aggressive policies of child support enforcement agencies. However, this stereotype overlooks the very real struggles many non-custodial parents face in trying to meet the demands of the system. Far from helping

children, the enforcement process can destroy the financial and emotional stability of non-custodial parents, leaving them trapped in a cycle of debt, poverty, and isolation. This chapter examines how the child support system unfairly penalizes these parents, often stripping them of their ability to contribute meaningfully to their children's lives.

1. Financial Strain and the Poverty Trap

For many non-custodial parents, child support payments represent a significant financial burden that can make it nearly impossible to escape poverty. The system's rigidity leaves no room for flexibility, even when parents face unexpected expenses, job loss, or other financial setbacks. As a result, child support payments can push non-custodial parents deeper into poverty.

Rigid Payment Requirements: The formula used to calculate child support obligations often fails to consider the financial reality of the non-custodial parent's life. Factors like fluctuating income, job instability, and essential expenses are disregarded, leaving many non-custodial parents unable to meet their obligations without sacrificing their own basic needs.

Cycle of Poverty: Once a non-custodial parent falls behind, penalties, interest, and fees begin to accumulate, making it nearly impossible to catch up. This financial burden can prevent them from accessing credit, buying a home, or building a stable future. The result is a perpetual poverty trap that leaves them with few options for improving their financial situation.

2. Mental Health Crisis Among Non-Custodial Parents

The stress of dealing with insurmountable debt and punitive enforcement measures has severe psychological effects on non-custodial parents. The constant threat of wage garnishment, legal penalties, and even jail time can lead to chronic anxiety, depression, and a sense of hopelessness. For some, the mental toll of child support enforcement is devastating.

Feelings of Hopelessness: Many non-custodial parents feel trapped in a system that offers no way out. With few avenues for relief, they often see their debt increase no matter how hard they work, leading to a profound sense of despair.
Social Isolation and Stigma: The societal stigma around unpaid child support often leaves non-custodial parents feeling isolated from their communities, friends, and even family members. This isolation can worsen mental health struggles, creating a vicious cycle that affects their ability to maintain stable employment or relationships.

3. Criminalization of Financial Hardship
One of the most harmful aspects of the child support enforcement system is its criminalization of poverty. Non-custodial parents who are unable to pay due to financial hardship are often treated as though they are willfully neglectful, when in reality, they are struggling to survive.

License Suspensions: License suspensions are a common enforcement tactic for unpaid child support. While intended as a deterrent, this measure often backfires by preventing non-custodial parents from getting to work or securing new employment, further reducing their ability to pay.
Jail Sentences for Non-Payment: In extreme cases, non-custodial parents can be jailed for unpaid child support, which is counterproductive for both the parent and the child. Imprisoning a parent for financial hardship not only prevents them from working but also places additional burdens on the taxpayer and

weakens family ties.

4. Barriers to Employment and Economic Mobility
The enforcement tactics used by child support agencies can create significant barriers to employment, trapping non-custodial parents in low-paying jobs with limited opportunities for advancement. These policies contradict the supposed goal of child support, as they actively reduce non-custodial parents' ability to earn a stable income.

Job Insecurity and Underemployment: Many non-custodial parents, particularly those with wage garnishments or licenses revoked, struggle to find or maintain employment. Employers may view these parents as financial risks or see their legal troubles as a distraction, limiting their job options.
Reduced Incentive to Work: For non-custodial parents facing high garnishment rates, the prospect of working can feel futile. If a large portion of their paycheck is seized before it even reaches them, they may lose motivation to work formally and instead seek under-the-table jobs to retain more of their earnings.

5. Impact on Family Relationships and Parenting
The relentless pursuit of child support payments often fractures family relationships. Non-custodial parents who are consistently penalized or stigmatized may feel resentment, not only toward the system but also toward their children or ex-partners, creating a toxic environment that undermines the child's emotional well-being.

Strained Parent-Child Relationships: The financial and emotional stress that non-custodial parents endure often hinders their ability to engage positively with their children. Some non-custodial parents may distance themselves from their children out of guilt, shame, or frustration, depriving children of meaningful relationships.

Resentment and Conflict with Custodial Parents: In many cases, the non-custodial parent may come to resent the custodial parent, viewing them as an enforcer rather than a partner in raising their children. This resentment can lead to conflict, making co-parenting arrangements difficult or even impossible.

6. Long-Term Consequences: A Lifetime of Debt and Limited Future

For many non-custodial parents, child support obligations become a lifelong burden. Even when children reach adulthood, accumulated arrears and interest can keep non-custodial parents in debt for years, sometimes for the rest of their lives. This perpetual debt cycle restricts their ability to rebuild, even when they are willing to do so.

Debt Beyond Child's 18th Birthday: Child support debt doesn't disappear when the child becomes an adult. In many cases, the non-custodial parent is required to continue payments on arrears, which can last indefinitely and restrict financial freedom long after children have left the household.

Limited Access to Financial Opportunities: With debt hanging over them, non-custodial parents often struggle to qualify for loans, rent apartments, or build savings. This lack of financial stability restricts their ability to contribute meaningfully to their families and to society, perpetuating cycles of poverty.

Conclusion: Abolition as a Path to Economic and Family Stability

The relentless financial and emotional strain placed on non-custodial parents by the child support enforcement system raises serious questions about its effectiveness. Rather than fostering a cooperative environment that supports both parents in raising their children, the current system perpetuates poverty, damages mental health, and fractures families. These impacts are not mere side effects—they are the direct results of a punitive and outdated approach.

Abolishing the child support enforcement system would allow for more humane, supportive solutions that do not criminalize parents for their financial situations. Programs aimed at providing employment support, income-based assistance, and family mediation would offer a healthier alternative to a system that currently punishes non-custodial parents without addressing the root causes of financial instability.

Only by dismantling the current child support model can society hope to create an environment where parents are empowered to support their children out of commitment, not compulsion. An approach based on partnership and mutual support would not only help non-custodial parents but also benefit the children and families who suffer under the current punitive system.

CHAPTER 5: EFFECT ON CHILDREN AND CUSTODIAL PARENTS

Introduction: The System's Failure to Support Families

The child support enforcement system was intended to benefit children by ensuring that non-custodial parents contribute financially to their upbringing. In practice, however, this system often creates additional hardship for children and custodial parents, the very people it is supposed to help. Instead of fostering a secure environment, the rigid, punitive structure of enforcement leaves custodial families vulnerable to financial instability, emotional strain, and ongoing conflict. This chapter explores how the enforcement system undermines the well-being of children and custodial parents, showing that the system does more harm than good and should be reconsidered entirely.

1. Financial Instability for Custodial Parents
While child support payments are meant to alleviate financial stress for custodial parents, the enforcement system often fails to deliver the promised stability. Custodial parents frequently experience delays, garnishments that fail to capture payments in full, and other administrative issues that prevent them from receiving consistent support.

Irregular and Unpredictable Payments: Despite the enforcement measures in place, many custodial parents find that payments are inconsistent or unreliable. The system's focus on punitive measures, rather than supportive solutions, means that non-custodial parents who are struggling financially may simply not be able to pay, leaving custodial parents without the support they need.
Costly Legal and Administrative Fees: Custodial parents are often required to navigate a bureaucratic maze of fees, legal paperwork, and court appearances just to secure basic support. The financial burden of these administrative costs can reduce the actual benefit of any child support payments, particularly for low-income custodial parents who cannot afford the added expenses.

2. Emotional and Psychological Toll on Children

One of the most significant but overlooked effects of child support enforcement is the emotional toll it takes on children. The system's punitive nature can create a toxic family environment where children feel caught between warring parents. Instead of fostering a supportive upbringing, the enforcement system often leads to resentment, stress, and broken family bonds.

Stress from Parental Conflict: Children are deeply affected by parental conflict, and the financial pressure imposed by the child support system often intensifies this conflict. Non-custodial parents may feel resentful and custodial parents may feel frustrated, creating an environment of tension that children can sense, even if they don't fully understand the situation.

Sense of Guilt and Burden: Many children feel guilty or burdened by their parents' struggles with child support payments. When children sense that they are the cause of financial stress, they may internalize this guilt, leading to anxiety, lowered self-esteem, and long-term psychological consequences.

◆ ◆ ◆

3. Reduced Quality of Life for Children
The punitive approach of child support enforcement does little to enhance the quality of life for children. In fact, the system often reduces the overall financial support that children receive, leaving custodial parents to shoulder the financial burden alone when enforcement efforts fall short.

Decreased Household Income: For custodial families, child support can be a critical source of income, but when non-custodial parents are subject to extreme enforcement actions, they may be left unable to pay consistently. This reduces the resources available for children's needs, undermining the system's primary purpose.

Economic Instability Due to Penalties: Enforcement actions like wage garnishments and license suspensions may push non-custodial parents to the point where they can no longer contribute financially, leaving custodial parents to struggle on their own. This is especially damaging for children in single-parent households who depend on child support to maintain basic needs.

4. Strain on Custodial Parents' Mental Health

Custodial parents often endure significant mental and emotional strain as they navigate the child support enforcement system. The pressure to secure payments, the constant stress of unpaid support, and the need to handle legal challenges can lead to chronic stress and mental health issues for custodial parents.

Anxiety and Financial Stress: Custodial parents frequently experience anxiety related to finances and uncertainty around child support payments. When payments are inconsistent or fail to come through, custodial parents are left to worry about covering bills, groceries, and other essentials.

Impact on Parenting: Chronic stress impacts a parent's ability to provide emotional support and stability for their children. Custodial parents dealing with child support issues may struggle to fully engage in parenting, leading to less quality time and attention for their children.

5. Disruption of Family Dynamics and Co-Parenting

The enforcement-centric approach of the child support system often drives a wedge between parents, making healthy co-parenting difficult, if not impossible. Custodial parents may become resentful of non-custodial parents who are unable to meet their obligations, leading to a breakdown in communication and cooperation.

Hostility and Resentment: When child support payments become a source of contention, both parents may become hostile toward each other, creating a hostile environment that children can sense and internalize. This animosity can last for years, making it difficult for parents to engage in cooperative co-parenting.

Isolation of the Non-Custodial Parent: Non-custodial parents often feel alienated from their children when they are pursued aggressively by the system. This isolation can lead to estranged relationships, leaving children with limited contact and support from one of their parents.

6. Inadequate Focus on the Best Interests of Children

The current child support enforcement system often prioritizes debt collection over the well-being of children. Instead of considering the needs of the child or the unique circumstances of each family, the system applies a blanket approach that can fail to address the specific needs of custodial families.

Failure to Address Family Needs Holistically: The enforcement system does not account for the full spectrum of a child's needs, such as emotional support, access to healthcare, or educational opportunities. By focusing solely on financial contributions, the system disregards other critical factors that contribute to a child's well-being.

Limited Support for Custodial Parents: Custodial parents who struggle financially are often left without adequate support from the government, even when child support payments are insufficient. Instead of providing comprehensive assistance, the system places the burden of enforcement on custodial parents, adding to their challenges without offering solutions.

Conclusion: A System That Fails Families

The child support enforcement system is failing to achieve its fundamental mission. Rather than providing stability, it creates more hardship for custodial parents and their children, fostering conflict, resentment, and financial instability. The unintended consequences of enforcement make it clear that this system is fundamentally flawed and cannot be reformed through minor adjustments alone.

Abolishing the current system would pave the way for a more supportive and flexible approach that genuinely addresses the needs of children and custodial parents. Direct financial assistance, community-based support programs, and job training initiatives for non-custodial parents are potential alternatives that could create a healthier environment for families. By shifting away from punitive enforcement and focusing on holistic family support, society can better serve the best interests of children and the parents who care for them.

The evidence is clear: the child support enforcement system does more harm than good for the families it is supposed to protect. Only by rethinking and replacing this system with compassionate, child-centered solutions can we ensure that children grow up in stable, supportive environments.

CHAPTER 6: LEGAL AND ETHICAL CONCERNS

Introduction: Questioning the Legitimacy of Child Support Enforcement

The child support enforcement system was created under the

premise of ensuring the welfare of children. However, a closer examination reveals that the current structure may violate basic principles of justice and fairness. From due process violations to punitive measures that criminalize poverty, the child support system operates in a way that would be deemed unacceptable in other legal contexts. This chapter argues that child support enforcement is not only flawed in practice but is fundamentally incompatible with constitutional protections and ethical norms.

1. Criminalization of Poverty

The most glaring ethical failure of the child support enforcement system is its tendency to criminalize financial hardship. Non-custodial parents who genuinely cannot afford to pay are treated as though they are criminals, subject to punitive actions that only worsen their financial situations.

Punishment for Economic Status: By using measures such as imprisonment, license suspensions, and garnishment of wages, the system effectively penalizes people for being poor. This approach is particularly unjust in cases where the non-custodial parent has made genuine efforts to secure employment but still cannot meet their child support obligations due to low wages or unstable work.

Violation of Equal Protection: The criminalization of poverty through child support enforcement creates a two-tiered justice system: one for the financially secure and another for the impoverished. Wealthier non-custodial parents are often able to meet their obligations, while low-income parents face severe penalties, demonstrating a lack of equal protection under the law.

2. Due Process Violations

Child support enforcement actions often infringe upon non-custodial parents' rights to due process. In some cases, parents face penalties without adequate notice, legal representation, or an opportunity to appeal. This lack of procedural fairness is a major legal flaw that further strengthens the case for abolishing the system.

Lack of Legal Representation: Many non-custodial parents cannot afford a lawyer, yet they are forced to navigate a complex legal system on their own. In cases where parents face jail time, the absence of legal representation is a violation of their constitutional rights, as they are effectively being deprived of their freedom without due process.

Arbitrary and Automatic Penalties: Child support enforcement relies heavily on automated systems that apply penalties without considering individual circumstances. This mechanized approach ignores the unique situations of each parent, treating them as mere numbers in a system rather than human beings with rights and dignity.

3. Excessive and Inhumane Punishments
The penalties imposed on non-custodial parents can be excessive, even draconian. Suspending a parent's driver's license or placing them in jail is not only disproportionate to the offense but also counterproductive, as it strips parents of their ability to earn income. The punitive nature of these measures raises serious ethical questions about the morality of a system that prioritizes punishment over rehabilitation.

License Suspensions and Employment Restrictions: Preventing a parent from working does nothing to ensure child support payments and instead exacerbates financial hardship. Ethical principles would suggest that any enforcement action should prioritize the well-being of the child and the family, yet punitive measures like license suspensions accomplish the opposite.

Imprisonment as a Means of Collection: Imprisoning parents for unpaid child support is ethically indefensible. This approach not only prevents parents from fulfilling their responsibilities but also places an additional burden on the state and taxpayers. Incarceration for non-payment is essentially a modern-day debtors' prison, a practice that was widely abolished for its inherent injustice.

4. Violations of Privacy and Personal Freedom

The child support enforcement system often invades the privacy of non-custodial parents, tracking their finances, employment, and even personal habits. This level of intrusion is typically reserved for individuals accused of serious crimes, yet it is applied broadly to parents struggling with financial hardship.

Surveillance of Financial Activity: Non-custodial parents are subjected to monitoring that allows the state to seize assets, garnish wages, and intercept tax refunds without their consent. This constant surveillance is an overreach of governmental authority, especially given that these parents have not committed any crime other than being unable to meet their obligations.

Loss of Personal Autonomy: When parents are unable to make independent financial decisions due to state-imposed restrictions and penalties, their personal freedom is effectively compromised. Ethical principles would demand that the state respect individuals' autonomy, yet the child support enforcement system disregards this by controlling aspects of parents' lives in ways that are inappropriate and unnecessary.

5. Disproportionate Impact on Marginalized Communities

The child support enforcement system disproportionately targets and impacts low-income and minority communities, perpetuating cycles of poverty and inequality. The racial and economic biases ingrained in the system make it not only ineffective but also unjust and discriminatory.

Racial Inequity in Enforcement: Studies have shown that Black and Latino non-custodial parents are disproportionately targeted for enforcement measures, such as wage garnishments, license suspensions, and incarceration. This racial bias highlights the unethical nature of a system that is supposed to be impartial but often exacerbates social inequalities.

Economic Discrimination: The system's design inherently punishes those who are economically disadvantaged, with harsher penalties and fewer avenues for relief. Instead of addressing poverty, child support enforcement perpetuates it, trapping marginalized communities in cycles of financial hardship that are difficult to escape.

6. Ignoring the Best Interests of Children

The enforcement system is supposedly designed to serve the best interests of children, but its punitive focus often achieves the opposite. By alienating non-custodial parents and undermining family stability, the system creates an environment that is detrimental to children's emotional and financial well-being.

Financial Instability for Children: When non-custodial parents are pushed into poverty, children do not receive the consistent financial support they need. Rather than enhancing children's quality of life, the system's punitive measures often reduce the financial resources available to them.

Emotional Harm from Parental Conflict: Children are deeply

affected by the conflict between parents, and the enforcement system intensifies this conflict. Instead of fostering a cooperative environment, the system's punitive nature drives parents apart, which can lead to emotional harm for children.

7. A System Rooted in Outdated and Punitive Ideals

The child support enforcement system's legal structure reflects an outdated worldview that sees non-custodial parents as morally deficient if they cannot meet their obligations. This system of judgment and punishment disregards the economic realities of today's workforce and treats parents as though they are criminals, even when they are struggling due to circumstances beyond their control.

Punishment vs. Rehabilitation: Ethical justice systems prioritize rehabilitation over punishment, yet the child support enforcement system has failed to evolve from its punitive roots. Instead of providing support, the system assigns blame, reinforcing harmful stereotypes that reduce parents to "deadbeats" rather than recognizing them as individuals facing real challenges.

A Legacy of Control and Oppression: The current system's origins in welfare reform have left it rooted in a mindset of control and punishment. By abolishing this system, society can move toward a more compassionate and equitable approach that respects the dignity and rights of all parents.

Conclusion: A Call for Justice and Ethical Reform

The child support enforcement system operates in ways that are fundamentally at odds with principles of justice, fairness, and human dignity. By criminalizing poverty, disregarding due process, imposing excessive punishments, and perpetuating inequality, the system fails to uphold the ethical standards expected in a fair and just society.

Abolishing this system would not only address these ethical and legal failures but would also open the door to more constructive solutions that prioritize the well-being of children and families. Instead of a punitive, one-size-fits-all approach, society could adopt policies that focus on economic support, rehabilitation, and family cooperation. Programs that provide job training, direct financial aid, and mental health support would better serve the true needs of families, creating a just and compassionate alternative to the current system.

The evidence is overwhelming: child support enforcement is legally questionable, ethically flawed, and fundamentally unjust. Abolishing it is the only way forward if we are to respect the rights, dignity, and humanity of all parents and create a society that genuinely cares for its children.

CHAPTER 7: THE FINANCIAL BURDEN ON SOCIETY

Introduction: An Inefficient and Costly System

The child support enforcement system is not only harmful to families but also astonishingly expensive for society. Despite billions of taxpayer dollars invested annually, the system produces limited benefits and creates massive administrative costs. For a system that claims to protect children, child support enforcement is failing at its mission while draining public resources that could be better allocated elsewhere. This chapter explores the financial burden of the enforcement system on taxpayers, citing government data to expose the inefficiency, waste, and unsustainable nature of this punitive approach.

1. The Cost of Enforcement: Billions Spent Annually
Child support enforcement is a multi-billion-dollar industry funded largely by taxpayer dollars. According to the federal Office of Child Support Enforcement (OCSE), the cost of running the child support program nationwide was approximately $5.7 billion in fiscal year 2020. This staggering figure covers enforcement actions, administrative expenses, legal fees, and the infrastructure required to monitor and collect payments from non-custodial parents.

Administrative Inefficiencies: Despite this significant investment, only a fraction of these funds reach the families who actually need support. A large portion of the budget goes toward administrative costs, which include wages for enforcement officers, legal fees, and technological infrastructure for tracking payments.
Limited Return on Investment: For every dollar spent on child support enforcement, OCSE reports a collection rate of approximately $5.06. While this might seem like a positive return, it pales in comparison to other social programs, especially when accounting for the immense human and societal costs associated with enforcement. These funds could be redirected to programs that provide direct aid to families without the need for coercive measures.

2. The High Cost of Incarceration for Non-Payment

Imprisoning parents for unpaid child support is a policy that many see as morally and financially indefensible. According to the Brennan Center for Justice, the average cost of incarcerating an individual in the United States is approximately $33,000 per year. For non-custodial parents who are jailed due to child support arrears, this cost falls entirely on the taxpayer, with no benefit to the child or custodial parent.

Counterproductive Spending: By incarcerating non-custodial parents, the state not only incurs a significant cost but also eliminates any chance of the parent generating income to support their children. This "solution" does nothing to solve the problem of unpaid support and actually creates additional burdens for society.

Lack of Revenue Generation: Unlike other forms of incarceration, jailing parents for non-payment generates no societal value. Instead, it adds to the cycle of poverty and costs taxpayers millions annually. Rather than imprisoning these individuals, funds could be used to create job programs and financial support services that would address the root causes of non-payment.

◆ ◆ ◆

3. Costly Enforcement Actions with Minimal Gains

Enforcement actions, such as wage garnishment, tax intercepts, and license suspensions, come with their own set of expenses. According to OCSE data, the cost of locating non-custodial parents, processing garnishments, and tracking payments can add up to thousands of dollars per case, with inconsistent results. In many cases, the funds spent on these actions exceed the amount of child support actually collected.

Tax Refund Intercepts: One common enforcement action is intercepting tax refunds from non-custodial parents. While this measure does lead to some collections, it is labor-intensive and costly. A report by the U.S. Department of Health and Human Services found that intercepting federal tax refunds is one of the most expensive forms of collection, often costing more than $30 per case for a single intercept attempt.

Driver's License Suspensions: Suspending driver's licenses for non-payment of child support is not only counterproductive but also expensive to administer. Processing license suspensions, reissuing licenses, and tracking compliance can add significant costs, all while reducing the likelihood of the non-custodial parent being able to find or maintain employment.

4. State and Local Budgets Strained by Enforcement

State and local governments bear a substantial share of child support enforcement costs. In many states, funding for child support programs comes from general revenue, meaning that taxpayer dollars intended for essential services are diverted to support enforcement efforts. This diverts resources from public services such as education, healthcare, and infrastructure, impacting the broader community.

Impact on Local Budgets: Local governments often rely on federal matching funds to support their child support programs. However, if they fail to meet certain quotas, these funds can be reduced, leaving states with additional financial strain. According to OCSE, some states spend over $500 million annually on child support enforcement, a cost that is ultimately passed on to taxpayers.

Lost Revenue from Ineffective Collection: Many non-custodial parents, especially those with low incomes, simply cannot meet the high demands imposed by child support orders. This results in millions of dollars in uncollected payments each year, meaning that enforcement actions are often futile, wasting taxpayer money with little to no return.

5. The Burden on Taxpayers: Funding a System That Doesn't Work
The high costs of enforcement actions, legal proceedings, and incarceration ultimately fall on taxpayers. Instead of creating financial stability for children, the current system siphons billions in public funds, leading many to question its effectiveness and sustainability. Taxpayer dollars should be directed toward programs that genuinely support families, not wasted on punitive measures that do little to improve children's lives.

The Debt Cycle and Taxpayer Liability: The enforcement system's heavy reliance on penalties and interest creates a cycle of debt that non-custodial parents cannot escape. As a result, a significant portion of child support debt goes uncollected, shifting the financial responsibility to taxpayers who fund public assistance programs for custodial parents who still require support.

Alternative Uses of Public Funds: Redirecting funds from child support enforcement to programs such as job training, direct financial assistance, and family counseling could provide more effective and compassionate support for families. By investing in these alternatives, society could reduce poverty, improve family stability, and create a more just and effective social support system.

6. The Real Cost of Emotional and Social Consequences
The financial burden of child support enforcement goes beyond dollars and cents; it has a human cost that affects society as a whole. Families torn apart by punitive enforcement measures create additional social problems, from mental health issues

to increased dependency on welfare programs. The cost of addressing these consequences is difficult to quantify, but it is clear that they represent a significant and often overlooked aspect of the system's true cost.

Increased Dependency on Social Services: Non-custodial parents who are financially devastated by enforcement measures often turn to public assistance programs just to survive. This dependency creates additional costs for social services, including housing, food assistance, and mental health care.

Generational Impact on Children: Children raised in environments marked by poverty and parental absence are more likely to require support as adults. By perpetuating poverty and family instability, the child support system creates an intergenerational cycle of dependency, further increasing the long-term cost to taxpayers.

7. A System That Costs More Than It Provides
The financial inefficiency of child support enforcement makes it clear that this system costs far more than it contributes to society. Billions are spent annually on enforcement, yet many families continue to struggle without the support they need. A system that prioritizes punishment over practical support is inherently unsustainable and offers little value for the money invested in it.

Unsustainable Spending Levels: The current spending on child support enforcement is unsustainable in the long run. With rising costs of legal fees, administrative processing, and incarceration, this system is becoming a drain on public resources. Continuing down this path without reform is economically irresponsible.

Minimal Impact on Child Welfare: Ultimately, the current system does little to enhance the well-being of children, the very individuals it claims to protect. For billions in spending, children deserve direct support, not a system that imposes hardships on their families and fails to provide meaningful assistance.

Conclusion: A Call to Abolish the Financially Unsustainable Enforcement System
The child support enforcement system is a financial burden on society, diverting billions in taxpayer dollars toward punitive measures that fail to provide meaningful support for families. Incarceration, administrative costs, and ineffective collection tactics make this system a costly failure that serves neither the children it purports to protect nor the taxpayers who fund it.

Abolishing the child support enforcement system would free up resources for programs that provide real, effective assistance to families. Direct financial aid, job training, mental health support, and family counseling would all be more cost-effective and compassionate alternatives, allowing society to invest in solutions that reduce poverty and improve family stability.

The data speaks for itself: child support enforcement is financially unsound, morally questionable, and fundamentally ineffective. It is time to abandon this outdated system and embrace solutions that truly benefit children and families.

CHAPTER 8: ALTERNATIVES TO PUNITIVE ENFORCEMENT

Introduction: A New Vision for Child Support

The current child support enforcement system, with its punitive focus, has proven ineffective and damaging to families. But abolishing this system doesn't mean abandoning the responsibility to support children. Instead, it offers an opportunity to explore innovative approaches that prioritize the well-being of children and families without imposing harsh penalties. This chapter examines alternative methods for securing financial stability and encouraging parental support, focusing on solutions that address the root causes of financial hardship and promote cooperation rather than punishment.

1. Income-Based Adjustments and Flexible Payment Plans
One of the most effective ways to support both children and parents is by implementing income-based adjustments for child support obligations. Under the current system, many non-custodial parents are ordered to pay amounts that are unrealistic given their income levels, often trapping them in a cycle of debt. By aligning payment obligations with a parent's actual income, the system could reduce arrears and improve compliance without resorting to punitive measures.

Realistic Payment Structures: Income-based payments ensure that non-custodial parents are not burdened by amounts they cannot realistically pay. For example, in countries like the United Kingdom, child support payments are calculated as a percentage of the non-custodial parent's income, with allowances for essential expenses.

Flexible Payment Plans for Hardship Cases: In cases of unemployment or other financial hardship, temporary payment reductions or deferrals could help parents avoid falling into arrears. By offering payment flexibility, the system can support parents during difficult periods without resorting to penalties or enforcement actions.

2. Direct Financial Assistance to Custodial Parents

Instead of relying on child support payments from non-custodial parents, direct financial assistance to custodial parents could provide a more reliable and effective way to ensure that children's needs are met. By establishing government-funded programs that offer monthly support to single-parent households, society can reduce poverty and provide a stable environment for children.

Universal Child Benefit Programs: Countries like Canada and Norway provide monthly child benefit payments to custodial parents, ensuring that children receive financial support regardless of the non-custodial parent's ability to pay. These programs are funded by the government and help to lift children out of poverty without punitive enforcement measures.

Supplemental Income Programs: Expanding programs like the Earned Income Tax Credit (EITC) in the United States could offer additional financial support to low-income custodial parents, helping them provide for their children without having to rely solely on child support payments.

3. Job Training and Employment Support Programs for Non-Custodial Parents

One of the main reasons for non-payment of child support is unemployment or underemployment among non-custodial parents. Rather than penalizing parents who are struggling to find work, a more effective approach would be to provide job training, employment assistance, and economic support tailored to their specific needs.

Skills Training and Certification Programs: Many non-custodial parents lack the skills or credentials needed for stable, well-paying jobs. Programs that offer training in high-demand fields, such as technology, healthcare, and skilled trades, could empower these parents to find better-paying jobs, making them more capable of supporting their children.

Work Incentives and Subsidized Employment: Programs that provide incentives for hiring non-custodial parents, such as wage subsidies or tax breaks for employers, could reduce unemployment among this group. By helping parents secure stable employment, these initiatives address the root cause of non-payment rather than punishing individuals for financial hardship.

4. Mediation and Collaborative Family Support Programs
The adversarial nature of the current child support enforcement system often creates hostility between parents, leading to fractured family relationships. By promoting mediation and cooperative support programs, the system could encourage parents to work together in the best interests of their children, fostering a more positive environment for co-parenting.

Mediation for Support Agreements: Mediation allows parents to reach their own agreements on support, custody, and visitation. This collaborative process can reduce resentment and encourage parents to work together, minimizing the need for court intervention. Research has shown that mediated agreements are often more successful and enduring than court-ordered arrangements.
Family Support Services: Programs that offer family counseling, parenting classes, and conflict resolution workshops can help parents navigate co-parenting challenges. By providing resources for families to resolve disputes and strengthen relationships, these services reduce the likelihood of conflict and enhance the stability of the family unit.

5. Child Support Insurance Models

An innovative approach to child support could involve establishing an insurance model, where parents contribute to a pooled fund that guarantees support payments in cases of financial hardship. This model would ensure that children receive consistent financial support without penalizing non-custodial parents who experience temporary financial setbacks.

Community-Based Insurance Programs: Similar to unemployment insurance, a child support insurance fund would allow non-custodial parents to contribute based on their income, with payments disbursed to custodial parents as needed. This model could be managed by a government agency or a non-profit organization, creating a safety net for children while reducing the financial pressure on individual parents.

Risk Pooling and Shared Responsibility: Insurance models operate on the principle of shared risk, spreading the financial burden across a larger pool of contributors. This approach could stabilize support payments for children and custodial parents, minimizing the impact of job loss or other financial crises on individual families.

6. Mental Health and Support Services for Parents

The current system neglects the mental health challenges many parents face due to the financial and emotional strain of child support enforcement. By offering mental health and support services for both custodial and non-custodial parents, society can create a more holistic support system that addresses underlying issues and improves family stability.

Therapeutic Support for Non-Custodial Parents: Many non-custodial parents experience depression, anxiety, and social stigma as a result of enforcement measures. Offering access to mental health services and counseling could help them cope with the emotional toll, making them more capable of maintaining employment and supporting their children.

Counseling for Custodial Parents: Custodial parents often face stress related to single parenting, financial insecurity, and conflict with the non-custodial parent. Providing counseling services for custodial parents can help them manage these challenges and ensure a more stable environment for children.

7. Community-Based Assistance and Support Networks
Building a community-based support network can provide families with the resources they need to thrive, regardless of child support enforcement. Local organizations, non-profits, and government programs can play a crucial role in offering assistance that directly addresses family needs without punitive oversight.

Food and Housing Assistance Programs: Many single-parent households struggle with food and housing insecurity. Expanding access to food assistance programs like SNAP and housing subsidies could provide a direct way to support custodial parents and children, reducing the need for child support as the sole financial lifeline.
Community Childcare and Educational Resources: Community centers and non-profit organizations could offer affordable childcare, after-school programs, and tutoring services. By providing access to these essential services, society can alleviate some of the financial pressure on custodial parents and promote a healthier, more supportive community environment for children.

Conclusion: A Path Toward Compassionate Support for Families

Abolishing punitive child support enforcement does not mean abandoning the responsibility to support children. Rather, it offers an opportunity to create a system that genuinely prioritizes children's well-being without harming parents in the process. By embracing alternatives such as income-based adjustments, direct financial assistance, employment programs, and community support networks, society can ensure that children have the resources they need while supporting parents in a constructive and humane manner.

The current child support enforcement system has shown itself to be costly, ineffective, and damaging to families. Shifting toward a supportive, compassionate approach could transform the way society supports families, creating healthier, more stable environments for children to thrive. By eliminating the punitive aspects of child support enforcement and focusing on practical, cooperative solutions, we can build a system that respects the dignity of all parents and ensures that no child is left without the support they deserve.

CHAPTER 9:
INTERNATIONAL MODELS
OF CHILD SUPPORT

Introduction: Learning from Global Perspectives

Around the world, child support systems vary widely, reflecting different cultural, economic, and political approaches to family welfare. Unlike the punitive system used in the United States, several countries have adopted models that emphasize income sensitivity, direct government support, and collaborative solutions. By examining these international approaches, we can explore alternatives that prioritize child welfare without imposing harsh penalties on parents. This chapter highlights a selection of global models that successfully provide for children's needs while reducing the adversarial nature of child support enforcement.

◆ ◆ ◆

1. Canada: The Income-Based Child Benefit System
Canada's approach to supporting children in single-parent households revolves around the Canada Child Benefit (CCB), a monthly payment provided directly to custodial parents based on household income. Instead of relying solely on child support from non-custodial parents, the CCB ensures that children receive consistent financial support regardless of the non-custodial parent's ability to pay.

Income-Adjusted Payments: The CCB is calculated based on the custodial parent's income, allowing low-income families to receive a larger monthly benefit. This approach ensures that children's needs are prioritized, without penalizing non-custodial parents for income fluctuations or employment challenges.

Reduction of Conflict and Enforcement Costs: Since the CCB is provided directly by the government, custodial parents don't have to rely solely on payments from non-custodial parents. This reduces conflict, eliminates the need for punitive enforcement actions, and minimizes administrative costs, creating a more stable environment for children.

◆ ◆ ◆

2. United Kingdom: The "Child Maintenance Service" and Self-Arranged Agreements

In the United Kingdom, parents are encouraged to reach their own arrangements regarding child support, known as "family-based arrangements," before involving government agencies. If parents cannot agree, they may use the Child Maintenance Service (CMS), a government agency that calculates child support based on the non-custodial parent's income but avoids punitive measures when possible.

Encouragement of Family-Based Arrangements: Approximately 49% of child support arrangements in the UK are made privately between parents, with no government intervention. This collaborative approach reduces conflict and allows parents to determine an arrangement that suits their specific needs.

Income-Based Calculation and Minimal Penalties: The CMS calculates payments based on a percentage of the non-custodial parent's income, with allowances for essential expenses and other children. If payments are missed, CMS first works with parents to establish a feasible payment plan rather than resorting to immediate punitive measures.

3. Australia: The Integrated Support and Assessment Model
Australia's child support system, managed by the Department of Human Services, emphasizes income-based assessments, flexibility, and government assistance. The system is designed to avoid punitive enforcement by working with parents to assess their financial capabilities and make realistic payment arrangements.

Income-Sensitive Calculations: Child support payments in Australia are calculated based on both parents' incomes and the number of nights the child spends with each parent. This model ensures a fair distribution of responsibility and takes into account the cost of shared custody arrangements.

Support Programs for Non-Custodial Parents: Instead of penalizing non-custodial parents who struggle to pay, Australia offers support programs that help them find employment, manage debt, and access mental health services. This approach is intended to keep parents engaged and capable of meeting their responsibilities, reducing the need for enforcement.

4. Norway: The State-Supported "Bidrag" System
Norway's child support system, known as Bidrag, includes government-managed payments that provide consistent support for children, with minimal dependence on non-custodial contributions. Instead of enforcing payments directly from non-custodial parents, the state provides a basic allowance to custodial parents, covering essential expenses for the child.

Government-Funded Child Support: Through the Norwegian National Insurance Scheme, custodial parents receive financial support from the state to ensure children's well-being. This removes the burden from non-custodial parents who may be struggling financially, while ensuring that children receive stable, reliable support.
Cooperative Parental Responsibility: Norway's child support model encourages parents to cooperate in raising their children, reducing the adversarial nature of child support by promoting shared responsibility rather than punitive measures.

5. Germany: The "Unterhaltsvorschuss" and State Advances
Germany operates a unique child support system known as Unterhaltsvorschuss, which provides custodial parents with

financial support directly from the government if the non-custodial parent cannot pay. The state then seeks reimbursement from the non-custodial parent but does not penalize them for genuine inability to pay.

Government Advances for Custodial Parents: If the non-custodial parent defaults on payments, the German government steps in to provide financial support to the custodial parent. This guarantees that children receive uninterrupted financial support, regardless of the non-custodial parent's situation.

Flexible Repayment Plans for Non-Custodial Parents: Instead of punitive measures, Germany's system allows non-custodial parents to negotiate realistic repayment plans with the government if they are unable to reimburse the full amount. This approach prevents parents from being overwhelmed by debt and promotes compliance without enforcement.

6. Sweden: Universal Child Allowance and Cooperative Parenting

Sweden's model, often seen as one of the most family-friendly systems in the world, emphasizes shared parental responsibility and government-supported child benefits. The Swedish Social Insurance Agency provides a universal child allowance to all families, ensuring that children receive consistent support regardless of parental financial status.

Universal Child Benefits: Sweden's universal child allowance is paid monthly to families to cover basic child-rearing costs. This system reduces dependence on non-custodial payments and ensures that every child receives a minimum level of financial support.

Parental Cooperation and Shared Custody: Swedish family

policies emphasize cooperative parenting and shared custody arrangements, reducing the need for child support enforcement. Government support allows parents to focus on co-parenting without financial conflict, creating a more stable and harmonious environment for children.

◆ ◆ ◆

7. Lessons from International Models: Reducing Conflict and Ensuring Stability

These international models highlight a common theme: child support systems that emphasize cooperation, government support, and income sensitivity are more effective at reducing conflict and ensuring that children's needs are met. By providing a foundation of financial support for children and offering flexible solutions for non-custodial parents, these systems avoid the adversarial nature of U.S. child support enforcement.

Reduced Dependence on Enforcement: Countries like Norway, Canada, and Sweden demonstrate that providing direct government support for children can reduce dependence on enforcement, creating a more reliable and less punitive system. When children's needs are met through universal or government-based benefits, there is less need for coercive enforcement actions that harm parents and families.

Income-Sensitive and Flexible Approaches: Income-sensitive calculations, as seen in the UK and Australia, allow child support obligations to adapt to parents' financial realities, reducing the likelihood of arrears and promoting consistent payments. By offering flexible payment arrangements, these countries have shown that cooperation is often more effective than punishment.

Conclusion: Adopting an International Perspective for Reform

The success of these international models underscores the need for the United States to adopt a new approach to child support that prioritizes children's welfare without punishing parents. By moving toward a model that combines government support, income-sensitive payments, and parental cooperation, the U.S. could establish a more humane and effective system that reduces family conflict and ensures financial stability for children.

Abolishing the punitive U.S. child support enforcement system would pave the way for an approach that aligns with best practices observed globally. Programs that offer direct assistance, flexible payment options, and community-based support could replace the need for harsh enforcement measures, creating a child support system that genuinely prioritizes the best interests of families. By embracing these global insights, the U.S. has an opportunity to transform a failing system into one that fosters stability, cooperation, and lasting support for children.

CHAPTER 10: ADVOCACY AND PUBLIC OPINION

Introduction: A Groundswell for Change
In recent years, the call to reform or abolish the punitive child support enforcement system has grown louder. Researchers, advocacy groups, and individuals affected by the system are increasingly vocal about its failures and the need for a more

compassionate, effective model. This chapter examines the rise in public awareness and support for change, fueled by evidence that punitive enforcement harms families more than it helps. By understanding the motivations and perspectives behind this movement, we gain insight into why reform—or outright abolition—is both necessary and achievable.

1. Advocacy Groups Leading the Charge

Several advocacy groups have taken up the cause of child support reform, drawing attention to the system's inherent flaws and proposing humane, family-centered alternatives. These organizations bring a range of perspectives, from criminal justice reform to economic justice, but all share a common goal: to end the punitive, counterproductive practices of child support enforcement.

National Parents Organization (NPO): The NPO advocates for shared parenting arrangements and reduced conflict in family court systems. They argue that cooperative parenting, rather than enforcement, is the key to ensuring children's financial and emotional well-being. The NPO actively promotes policies that reduce the adversarial nature of child support.

The Brennan Center for Justice: This criminal justice reform organization has published studies on the financial burden of incarcerating parents for non-payment, highlighting the need to decriminalize poverty. Their research provides evidence that punitive child support enforcement only deepens cycles of poverty, urging policymakers to reconsider harsh penalties and invest in support-oriented solutions.

2. Researchers and Economists Expose Systemic Inefficiencies

Academics and economists have contributed significantly to the growing understanding that the current child support system is economically inefficient and socially harmful. Studies from reputable institutions highlight the financial and human costs associated with enforcement, calling for systemic change.

Studies on the Cost of Incarceration: Research from organizations like the Vera Institute of Justice demonstrates that jailing parents for unpaid child support is financially wasteful and counterproductive. The cost of incarcerating a non-violent, non-custodial parent averages around $33,000 per year, while this measure does nothing to improve child support payments for families.

Analysis of Child Support Debt: Economists point out that a large proportion of child support arrears are owed by low-income parents who simply cannot afford to pay. Studies show that around 70% of child support debt is owed by parents earning less than $10,000 a year. These findings make a compelling case for income-based payments and flexible support structures over punitive enforcement.

3. Testimonials from Affected Parents

Personal stories from both custodial and non-custodial parents reveal the emotional and financial toll of child support enforcement. These testimonials provide a human face to the issue, showing how real families are impacted by the system's rigid structure and harsh penalties.

Non-Custodial Parents' Struggles: Many non-custodial parents describe feeling trapped in a cycle of debt, with interest and penalties accumulating faster than they can pay. For some, the stress and financial pressure of child support enforcement have led to job loss, homelessness, and severe mental health struggles.

Their stories highlight the need for compassionate reform and alternatives to enforcement.

Custodial Parents Seeking Stability: While custodial parents want financial support for their children, many are increasingly aware that punitive enforcement doesn't solve the underlying issues. Some custodial parents advocate for government assistance or direct aid to stabilize family finances rather than relying on an unpredictable, adversarial system.

4. Public Opinion Shifts Toward Reform

Surveys and public opinion polls indicate a shift in how the public views the child support enforcement system. The traditional view of "deadbeat" parents is giving way to a more nuanced understanding of the challenges faced by non-custodial parents, especially those with low incomes. Many people now support income-based adjustments and more supportive approaches that focus on the well-being of children without punishing parents for financial hardship.

Growing Sympathy for Low-Income Non-Custodial Parents: According to recent surveys, a majority of Americans believe that child support payments should be adjusted based on a parent's income level. This public support for income-based adjustments reflects a broader understanding of economic inequality and a rejection of the punitive measures that disproportionately impact the poor.

Support for Direct Child Assistance Programs: Many Americans support the idea of providing direct financial assistance to custodial parents through government programs, similar to the child tax credit or SNAP benefits. By reducing reliance on non-custodial payments, these programs could reduce family conflict and ensure that children receive consistent support.

5. Legislative Efforts and Policy Proposals
Recognizing the need for reform, several lawmakers and policymakers are beginning to propose changes to the child support system. These proposals, though varied, indicate a growing acknowledgment within government circles that punitive enforcement is not serving families effectively.

Income-Based Child Support Bills: Some states are exploring legislation that would allow child support obligations to be based on non-custodial parents' income levels, rather than flat-rate payments. This shift could alleviate financial strain for low-income parents, improve compliance, and reduce arrears, leading to better outcomes for families.

Alternatives to Incarceration: Several states have introduced bills aimed at eliminating jail time as a penalty for unpaid child support. Instead, these bills propose alternatives such as community service, job training, or temporary reductions in payments during periods of unemployment. These changes aim to keep parents engaged in the workforce rather than criminalizing them for financial hardship.

6. The Role of Media in Shaping Public Perception
Media coverage of child support enforcement issues has played a significant role in shifting public opinion. News outlets and documentaries have highlighted the human impact of enforcement measures, from homelessness to incarceration, making it clear that the current system often exacerbates poverty rather than alleviates it.

Documentaries and Investigative Reports: Documentaries such as "Where's Daddy?" and investigative reports by major media outlets have brought child support issues into the spotlight, revealing the cycle of poverty and punishment that the system perpetuates. These media portrayals give voice to affected families and showcase the need for reform.

Social Media and Grassroots Advocacy: Social media has given affected parents a platform to share their experiences, forming a grassroots movement that calls for change. Hashtags like #ChildSupportReform and #EndDebtorsPrison have helped raise awareness and create a community of advocates who demand a more humane and effective child support system.

Conclusion: A Movement Gaining Momentum
The call to abolish or reform the child support enforcement system is no longer a fringe issue. Advocates, researchers, parents, and the public at large are recognizing that punitive enforcement fails to address the core needs of families and, in many cases, worsens their financial and emotional burdens. The movement for change is supported by data, personal stories, and a shifting public opinion that increasingly favors compassionate, realistic solutions over punishment.

This growing consensus reflects a society that values family stability, economic fairness, and the well-being of children. By abolishing the current enforcement model and adopting a more supportive, family-centered approach, we can create a system that genuinely helps families thrive. Public opinion, backed by advocacy and research, makes it clear that punitive enforcement is outdated, ineffective, and ready to be replaced with solutions that prioritize cooperation, compassion, and real support for children and parents alike.

CHAPTER 11: PROPOSED FRAMEWORK FOR A REFORMED SYSTEM

Introduction: Building a System That Supports Families
Abolishing the punitive child support enforcement system doesn't mean abandoning the responsibility to support children. Instead, it opens the door to a new framework that genuinely meets the needs of children, custodial parents, and non-custodial parents alike. This chapter outlines a proposed framework for a reformed child support system—one that provides reliable

financial assistance, addresses underlying issues of poverty and employment, and prioritizes collaboration over punishment. By embracing these elements, society can ensure that children receive the support they deserve in a way that strengthens families rather than fracturing them.

1. Income-Based Payment Calculations

One of the most important changes in a reformed child support system would be adopting income-based payment calculations. Unlike the current model, which imposes rigid payment obligations regardless of a parent's income, an income-based system would tailor obligations to each parent's financial situation, increasing the likelihood of compliance and reducing the risk of debt.

Flexible, Percentage-Based Payments: Similar to models in the UK and Australia, a reformed system could calculate payments as a percentage of the non-custodial parent's income, with allowances for basic living expenses. This would ensure that parents aren't forced into poverty to meet unrealistic obligations.

Automatic Adjustments for Income Changes: If a parent's income fluctuates due to job loss, medical expenses, or other financial hardships, the payment obligation could automatically adjust. This approach would eliminate the need for constant court interventions and reduce the likelihood of accumulating arrears.

2. Government-Supported Child Benefits

A successful child support framework doesn't rely solely on contributions from non-custodial parents. Government-supported child benefits would provide a consistent financial base for custodial parents, ensuring that children's needs are met even when non-custodial parents face economic hardship. This model has been successful in Canada and several European countries, reducing reliance on enforcement while promoting financial stability for children.

Universal Child Allowance: Providing a monthly child benefit to custodial parents, regardless of their income, would create a reliable foundation of support for children. This direct assistance would help cover essentials such as housing, food, and education, minimizing financial stress for single-parent households.

Supplemental Child Support for Low-Income Families: For families below the poverty line, a supplemental child benefit could provide additional assistance, helping custodial parents avoid reliance on unpredictable or inconsistent payments from non-custodial parents.

3. Employment and Training Programs for Non-Custodial Parents

Rather than punishing non-custodial parents who are struggling financially, a reformed system would focus on employment support. By providing job training, educational programs, and employment resources, the system could address the root causes of non-payment, empowering parents to meet their obligations.

Job Training and Certification Programs: Many non-custodial parents lack the skills needed for stable, well-paying employment. Programs offering training in high-demand fields—such as healthcare, technology, and skilled trades—would enable these parents to secure better jobs and reliably support their children.

Work Incentives and Subsidized Employment: Government-funded work incentives and partnerships with employers could increase job opportunities for non-custodial parents, especially those with low incomes. Subsidized employment programs, such as wage supplements, would help ensure that parents can afford to meet their child support obligations.

4. Mediation and Family Support Services

A family-centered approach to child support would prioritize cooperation and communication over adversarial enforcement. Mediation and support services could help parents work together to create support agreements that suit their unique family dynamics, reducing conflict and promoting a stable environment for children.

Cooperative Mediation for Support Agreements: In a reformed system, parents would be encouraged to reach mutually agreed-upon arrangements through mediation. This approach has been shown to reduce animosity and foster cooperation, creating an environment where both parents feel invested in supporting their child's well-being.

Family Counseling and Conflict Resolution: Family counseling services and conflict resolution workshops could help parents navigate co-parenting challenges. By addressing conflicts and fostering communication, these services would enable parents to collaborate rather than resorting to court battles, which often deepen family tensions.

5. Income-Adjusted Repayment Plans for Arrears

Under the current system, child support arrears accumulate rapidly, trapping many parents in debt cycles they cannot escape. A reformed framework would introduce income-adjusted repayment plans that allow parents to realistically pay down arrears without facing overwhelming penalties and interest charges.

Interest-Free Payment Plans for Low-Income Parents: In cases where arrears have accumulated due to genuine financial hardship, parents could access interest-free repayment plans. This approach would enable parents to gradually pay down debt while avoiding further financial strain.

Debt Forgiveness for Long-Term Arrears: For parents with long-standing arrears that they are unlikely to repay, the system could offer debt forgiveness programs. By reducing or eliminating unmanageable debt, the system would allow parents to focus on consistent support payments moving forward rather than feeling overwhelmed by past obligations.

6. Mental Health and Social Support Services

A truly supportive child support system would recognize the mental and emotional challenges faced by both custodial and non-custodial parents. Mental health services and social support resources could help parents manage the emotional stress of single parenting and financial hardship, fostering a healthier family environment.

Therapeutic Support for Non-Custodial Parents: For non-custodial parents who face anxiety, depression, or other mental health challenges due to enforcement pressures, accessible mental health services could make a significant difference. Counseling, therapy, and support groups would help parents regain stability and improve their capacity to meet obligations.

Counseling and Resource Centers for Custodial Parents: Custodial parents, especially those navigating single parenting, would benefit from counseling and resource centers that offer financial advice, parenting support, and mental health resources. By helping custodial parents build stability, these services would directly benefit children's well-being.

7. Direct Financial Assistance for Children's Educational and Health Needs

A reformed system could provide direct financial assistance for children's educational and healthcare needs, reducing the pressure on both custodial and non-custodial parents to cover these essential expenses. By ensuring that children's basic needs are met, society can create a foundation for healthier and more stable family dynamics.

Educational Grants and Scholarships: Government-provided educational grants or scholarships for children from single-parent households would ensure access to quality education, regardless of a parent's ability to pay child support. This could help bridge the gap in resources and promote equal opportunities for children.

Subsidized Healthcare and Insurance for Children: Providing healthcare subsidies or insurance coverage for children in single-parent families would alleviate a significant financial burden. This direct support would ensure that children receive necessary medical care without placing an excessive financial strain on their parents.

8. Community-Based Support and Networking Programs

A reimagined child support system would include community-based support networks, enabling families to access resources, build social connections, and develop stronger support systems within their communities. By empowering communities to support families, the system can foster resilience and reduce the need for government intervention.

Community Resource Centers for Single Parents: Community resource centers could offer essential services such as childcare, job placement assistance, and family counseling, creating a local support network for single-parent households. These centers would reduce isolation and provide a safety net for families in need.

Parenting and Mentorship Programs: Connecting custodial and non-custodial parents with mentors or peer support groups could help them navigate the challenges of single parenting, improving outcomes for children and promoting family stability. Community-based mentorship fosters personal growth, accountability, and social connection.

Conclusion: A Path Toward Real Support for Families

The punitive child support enforcement model has failed to serve families effectively. In contrast, a reformed child support system that prioritizes flexibility, government assistance, and community support offers a practical, humane alternative. By embracing income-based payments, mental health services, job training, and direct support for children, society can create a system that truly meets the needs of families and improves children's lives.

This proposed framework represents a shift from punishment to partnership, from conflict to cooperation. Such a system would empower both custodial and non-custodial parents, fostering financial stability and family harmony. Abolishing punitive enforcement is the first step toward building a child support system that genuinely supports families and paves the way for a future where children grow up in secure, loving environments.

CHAPTER 12: CONCLUSION —THE CASE FOR CHANGE

A Broken System in Need of Abolition

The child support enforcement system, originally designed to ensure that children receive financial support, has evolved into a punitive, adversarial, and often counterproductive institution. By prioritizing enforcement and punishment over support, the system has imposed a severe burden on non-custodial parents, destabilized families, and, tragically, often failed to deliver consistent financial assistance to children. From crushing debt and punitive penalties to counterproductive enforcement practices, it's clear that this system does more harm than good.

This book has examined the ways in which child support enforcement undermines its own purpose, creating financial hardship, conflict, and emotional distress for families. It has highlighted the mounting public and expert support for reform, inspired by a belief that children and parents alike deserve a system rooted in compassion, understanding, and practical solutions. The time has come to move beyond enforcement and explore real alternatives that empower families to thrive.

The Arguments for Abolition: A Recap
Throughout the book, several key reasons for abolishing the current child support system have emerged. Here are the most compelling arguments:

Criminalization of Poverty: The system's punitive measures, including wage garnishments, license suspensions, and even incarceration, criminalize financial hardship and trap low-income parents in cycles of debt. By penalizing poverty, the system only worsens the financial strain on families and does nothing to benefit children.

Inadequate Support for Children: The current model often fails to provide consistent financial stability for children. Custodial parents experience delays, erratic payments, and administrative costs that undermine their ability to depend on child support as a reliable source of income.

Destructive Impact on Family Relationships: The adversarial nature of enforcement exacerbates conflict between parents, pushing them further apart and creating an environment of resentment and distrust. Children become collateral in these conflicts, facing emotional distress from divided family relationships.

Financial Burden on Society: The costs of enforcing child support —administrative expenses, legal fees, and incarceration—add up to billions in taxpayer dollars each year. This financial burden is unsustainable, especially given that the funds often fail to improve children's well-being. Redirecting these resources could offer greater value to society by supporting families directly.

Violation of Basic Rights and Justice: The enforcement system operates with little regard for due process or equal treatment. By suspending licenses, garnishing wages, and jailing parents without considering individual circumstances, the system disregards fundamental principles of fairness and justice.

Growing Public Demand for Change: Advocacy groups, researchers, and the general public increasingly support income-based adjustments, government-backed child benefits, and community support as viable alternatives to the current enforcement model. This groundswell of support reflects a widespread understanding that punitive enforcement is not the answer.

A Vision for a Compassionate Alternative
Abolishing the current enforcement system does not mean abandoning the responsibility to support children. On the contrary, it creates an opportunity to build a new model that genuinely prioritizes family welfare. The vision for a reformed child support system is one that balances flexibility, fairness, and direct assistance to provide reliable, meaningful support to children without punishing parents.

Income-Based Payments: Adopting flexible, income-sensitive payment structures that adjust to non-custodial parents' financial situations would ensure that child support obligations are realistic and sustainable.

Government-Supported Child Benefits: Providing a guaranteed minimum child allowance through government support would offer children and custodial parents reliable financial security, reducing the need for reliance on non-custodial contributions alone.

Job Training and Employment Support: Empowering non-custodial parents to improve their employment prospects and earning capacity is a more sustainable and supportive approach than penalizing them for unemployment or low income.

Mental Health and Family Support Services: Offering counseling, family mediation, and mental health services would support parents in overcoming the emotional and psychological challenges of single parenting, reducing family conflict and promoting healthier relationships.

Direct Assistance for Children's Needs: Providing educational grants, healthcare subsidies, and community-based resources would help ensure that children's essential needs are met regardless of parental income.

The Call for Systemic Change
The arguments for abolishing the current child support enforcement system are compelling, grounded in both the harm caused by punitive measures and the potential for a more effective, compassionate model. By replacing punishment with support, society can better serve families, reduce poverty, and foster healthier, more stable environments for children.

Each component of the proposed reformed system has been successfully implemented in various international models, demonstrating that a cooperative, family-centered approach is not only possible but also effective. Nations that prioritize direct child benefits, income-based support structures, and government assistance have reported better outcomes for children and families, proving that support is a more viable and ethical solution than enforcement.

Moving Forward: Advocacy and Action
The journey to abolish punitive child support enforcement requires ongoing advocacy, education, and legislative action. Public awareness is key to challenging longstanding misconceptions about non-custodial parents and the punitive nature of child support. By sharing personal stories, amplifying research, and engaging policymakers, advocates for reform can drive the momentum needed to achieve meaningful change.

Legislative Reforms: Lawmakers at the local, state, and federal levels must be encouraged to introduce and support bills that reduce or eliminate punitive child support enforcement practices. Policies that prioritize income-based adjustments, government benefits, and non-enforcement alternatives can gradually pave the way for systemic change.

Community Support and Resources: Community organizations, non-profits, and support networks can play a crucial role in providing resources for single-parent families, offering direct support that reduces dependency on enforcement while building a foundation for family stability.

Continued Research and Public Education: Ongoing research into the effects of punitive enforcement on families and the benefits of supportive models will provide evidence-based arguments to support abolition. Educational campaigns can also shift public opinion, helping to break down stigma and promote understanding of the challenges faced by non-custodial parents.

A New Future for Families

By embracing a model rooted in compassion, fairness, and collaboration, society can finally address the root causes of financial hardship for families and create a system that truly prioritizes children's needs. The ultimate goal of child support should be to provide stability, not punishment. By abolishing the current enforcement model and building a reformed system, we can create a future where every child grows up in a secure, supportive environment—one where parents are empowered, not punished, and where children's well-being is genuinely at the heart of the system.

The time for change is now. The evidence is clear, and the voices calling for reform are growing louder. Together, we can create a new path for child support, one that respects the dignity of all parents and ensures that no child is left without the support they deserve.

www.ingramcontent.com/pod-product-compliance
Lightning Source LLC
Chambersburg PA
CBHW061258250726
48653CB00002B/677